MARY
and the
GARDENER

written by
Paul Kerensa

illustrated by
Leanne Daphne

beaming ☀ books
MINNEAPOLIS

Copyright © 2025 Beaming Books. All rights reserved.
No part of this book may be reproduced without the written permission of the publisher. Email copyright@beamingbooks.com.

30 29 28 27 26 25 24   1 2 3 4 5 6 7 8

Hardcover ISBN: 979-8-8898-3485-4
eBook ISBN: 979-8-8898-3486-1

Library of Congress Control Number: 2024943105 (print)

Beaming Books
PO Box 1209
Minneapolis, MN 55440-1209
Beamingbooks.com

Printed in China.

Once, long ago, there was a man and a woman in a garden.

No, it's not **THAT** story in a garden.
It wasn't called Eden, he wasn't called Adam,
she wasn't called Eve, there was no snake.

But there was a tree.

The woman was called Mary,
and in the corner of the garden,
by the entrance to a tomb, she sat crying.

Crying, because Jesus had died.

She looked into the tomb, where Jesus's body was meant to be.

But there was no body. Instead, there was a vision of light around the stone slab, and a voice behind her.

"Why are you crying?"

She turned to see a man—the Gardener. "Who are you looking for?" he asked.

Mary was comforted as she remembered the man she was looking for.

A great teacher, Jesus healed and worked miracles.

He spoke of peace and hope for a brighter future.

"I am here to visit his body," Mary explained. "They've taken him away! I don't know where they put him."

The Gardener gave no words, but looked on kindly as he scattered seeds across the garden.

Mary smiled. It reminded her of a story that Jesus used to tell: the Parable of the Sower, about a man scattering grain. Some seeds grew, some did not— but still he scattered.

Like the Sower's seeds, our own seeds of faith, love, and kindness may or may not grow in others' lives.

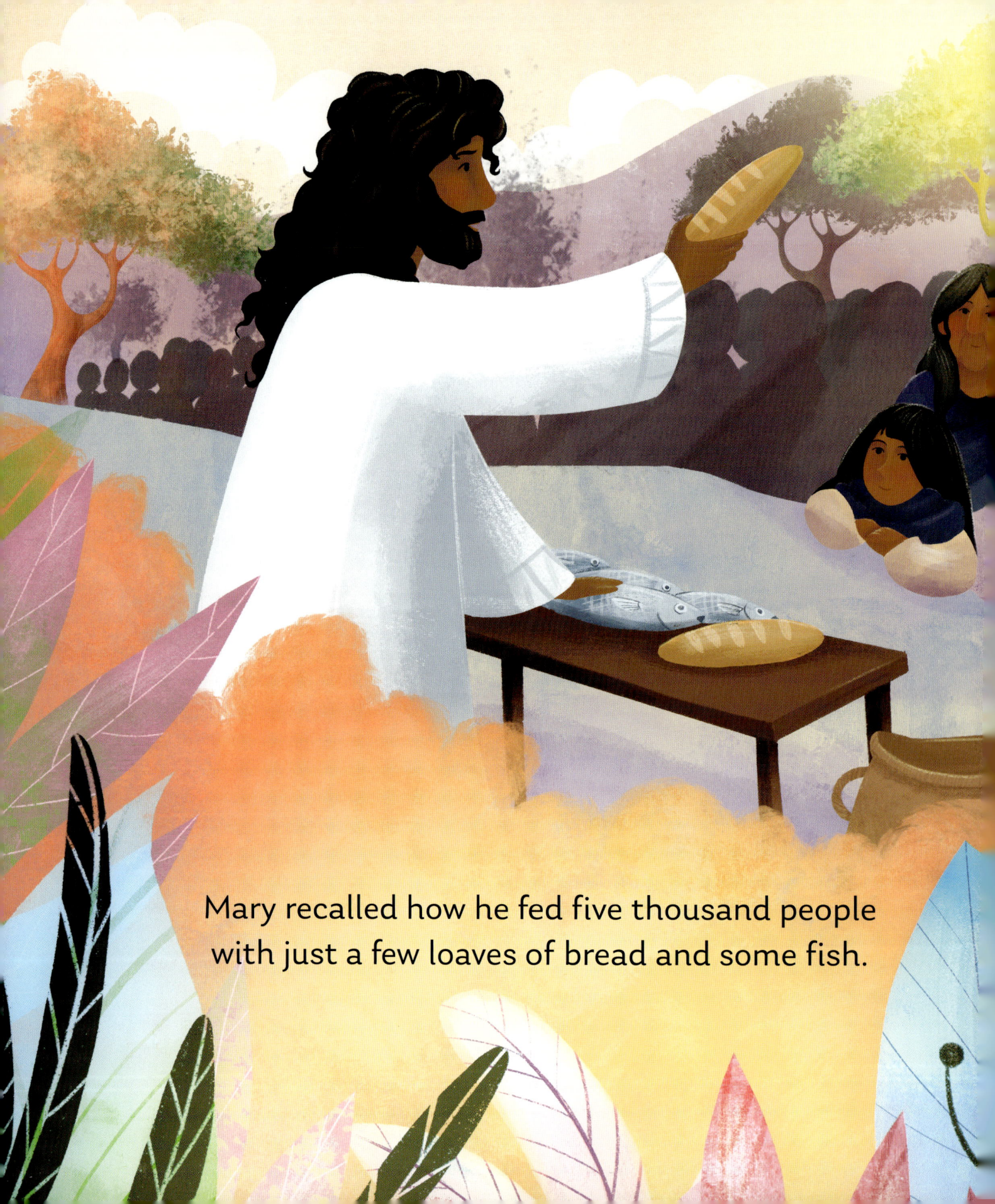
Mary recalled how he fed five thousand people with just a few loaves of bread and some fish.

She remembered how he showed kindness to people who were left out. How he made sure everyone was fed, and no one went hungry.

Soon he was praised with palm leaves, like the leaves in this garden.

He was in a different garden a few days later, where he was arrested by soldiers.

And a tree, like this garden's trees, was felled and carved into a cross.

Mary couldn't believe her teacher and friend was gone. She began to sob. The Gardener comforted her.

"After he died, Jesus was taken here," she said. "His body should be here! In this tomb!"

"If this is your garden, have you carried him somewhere? Where is he? Tell me, I'll go and get him!"

"Mary!" said the Gardener, with the kindest voice you can imagine.

At the sound of her name, Mary's last tear fell to the ground.

"Go and tell others," said the Gardener.

Mary was the first to see him.
She would be the first to share the good news too!

Jesus, the Gardener. Alive, once again.

Mary raced out of the garden to tell her friends. When she looked back, she saw plants blooming as he threw more seed.

"Come see! Jesus is alive!" she shouted to all who could hear, scattering her words far and wide.

Like his seeds, Mary's words would spread and grow into something bigger.

Like that other garden story—of Eden, and Adam and Eve and the fruit—this was also about a new start.

A new start for Mary—and a new start for you and me.

It starts with a garden.
And it's all thanks to the Gardener.

Paul Kerensa is a British Comedy Award-winning writer who has written for TV and radio. Paul teaches comedy writing for BBC Writer's Room and the London Screenwriters' Festival.

Leanne Daphne is an illustrator and world builder. She draws inspiration from the natural world and specializes in creating landscapes, unique characters, flora, and fauna that capture the imagination and tell a compelling story.